PRACTICAL
HORS d'OEUVRE
AND CANAPÉ ART

# PRACTICAL HORS d'OEUVRE AND CANAPÉ ART

A Pictorial Presentation of Foodservice Specialties

Charles Mok

CBI Publishing Company, Inc.
51 Sleeper Street
Boston, Massachusetts 02210

**Library of Congress Cataloging in Publication Data**

Mok, Charles.
   Practical hors d'oeuvre and canape art, a
   pictorial presentation of foodservice
   specialties.

   1. Cookery (Appetizers)   I. Title.
TX740.M58   641.8'12   78-1066
ISBN  0-8436-2159-1

Copyright © 1978 by CBI Publishing Company, Inc.
All rights reserved. No part of this book may be
reproduced in any form without express written
permission from the publisher.

Printed in the United States of America

Photography by Amy H. Lui

# TABLE OF CONTENTS

INTRODUCTION  vii
ABOUT THE AUTHOR  viii
BASIC TOOLS FOR PREPARATION  viii
BASIC INGREDIENTS CHECKLIST  ix

## COLD HORS d'OEUVRES

### SEAFOOD VARIATIONS

| | |
|---|---|
| Caviar Concert | 1-C |
| Cherry Stone Clam | 1-B |
| Clam Royale | 1-J |
| Crab Finger | 1-A |
| Escargots en Brochette | 1-E |
| Lobster Medallion | 1-L |
| Mushroom Button Garni | 1-K |
| Mussel Diable | 1-H |
| Oyster on the Half Shell | 1-G |
| Raw Tuna | 1-F |
| Scallop Delicia | 1-D |
| Shrimp Cocktail | 1-I |

### MEAT AND POULTRY VARIATIONS

| | |
|---|---|
| Chicken Plantation | 3-G |
| Chopped Liver Surprise | 3-E |
| Corned Beef Swirl | 3-I |
| Deli Sombrero | 3-H |
| Ham 'n' Asparagus Roll | 3-F |
| Marinated Beef Cube | 3-J |
| Marinated Chicken Liver | 3-K |
| Melon Cornet | 3-A |
| Petite Beef Roulade | 3-D |
| Smoked Tongue Treat | 3-B |
| Steak Tartare | 3-L |
| Turkey Cornet | 3-C |

### EGG AND CHEESE VARIATIONS

| | |
|---|---|
| Anchovy and Egg | 5-A |
| Athenea | 5-B |
| Bird of Paradise | 5-J |
| Blue Gem | 5-G |
| Caspian Egg | 5-D |
| Egg Diable | 5-F |
| Ham and Egger | 5-H |
| Kaleidoscope | 5-K |
| Miniature Egg | 5-C |
| Star-Top | 5-L |
| Stellar Cheddar | 5-E |
| Strawberry Delight | 5-I |

### VEGETABLE VARIATIONS

| | |
|---|---|
| Artichoke Pheasant | 7-A |
| Carrot-Olive Stuffer | 7-J |
| Celery Stuffer | 7-L |
| Cherry Bomb | 7-I |
| Ham and Cucumber Wedge | 7-E |
| Heart of Palm with Prosciutto | 7-D |
| Mushroom Cap with Avocado | 7-K |
| Radish Planter | 7-C |
| Stuffed Artichoke Bottom | 7-F |
| Tomato Boat | 7-G |
| Water Chestnut Surprise | 7-H |
| Western Star | 7-B |

### MISCELLANEOUS

| | |
|---|---|
| Calves' Brains Surprise | 9-D |
| Crab Finger Boat | 9-F |
| Goose Liver Roulade | 9-C |
| Ham and Cuke Carousel | 9-B |
| Hunter's Pride | 9-G |
| Lox and Cream Cheese | 9-H |
| Mushroom Brochette | 9-A |
| Olive and Avocado | 9-E |
| Prosciutto and Lemon | 9-I |
| Seafood Diable | 9-L |
| Sweetbread 'n' Artichoke | 9-K |
| Tomato Topper | 9-J |

## COLD CANAPÉS

### SEAFOOD VARIATIONS

| | |
|---|---|
| Anchovy Ring | 13-G |
| Baby Shrimp Canape | 13-L |
| Caviar Canape | 13-H |
| Crab Log Canape | 11-G |
| Crabmeat Canape | 13-D |
| Deviled Clam | 11-D |
| Escargot Surprise | 13-J |
| Gefilte Fish Canape | 13-F |
| Jumbo Shrimp | 11-L |
| Lobster Salad | 13-E |
| Lobster Tail Canape | 11-F |
| Lox and Cream Cheese Swirl | 13-I |
| Marinated Gefilte Fish | 11-I |
| Marinated Herring | 11-B |
| Red Caviar Canape | 11-K |
| Salmon Rose | 11-A |
| Salmon Salad Canape | 13-C |
| Sardine Canape | 11-J |
| Shrimp Salad Canape | 13-A |
| Smoked Baby Clams | 11-H |
| Smoked Oyster | 11-E |
| Smoked Salmon Spread | 11-C |
| Smoked Sturgeon | 13-K |
| Tuna Salad Canape | 13-B |

*continued*

# COLD CANAPÉS
*continued*

## MEAT AND POULTRY VARIATIONS

| | |
|---|---|
| Bar-B-Q Beef Delight | 17-A |
| Beef and Salad Log | 15-A |
| Canadian Caper | 17-L |
| Fantasy of Ham | 17-I |
| For Liver Lovers | 15-I |
| Ham and Pickle Roll | 17-E |
| Ham and Swisser | 15-G |
| Ham Canape | 17-D |
| Headcheese Pyramid | 17-B |
| Liver and Egg | 17-C |
| Meat Ball Hero | 17-H |
| Pastrami Special | 15-L |
| Perky Turkey | 15-H |
| Petite Sausage and Cheese | 17-K |
| Pineapple and Chicken | 17-F |
| Piquant Beef | 17-J |
| Pow Wow | 15-J |
| Smoked Ham Log Jam | 15-B |
| Smoked Sausage and Slaw | 15-K |
| Smoked Tongue Special | 15-D |
| Spotted Butterfly | 15-F |
| Turkey-Carrot Combo | 17-G |
| Turkey Club Canape | 15-E |
| Turkey Lily | 15-C |

## VEGETABLE VARIATIONS

| | |
|---|---|
| Almondine | 19-D |
| Artichoke Bottom St. Germaine | 19-B |
| Avocado Terrace | 19-K |
| Carrotique | 19-L |
| Corn Crib | 19-F |
| Mushroomique | 19-J |
| Normandy | 19-I |
| Princess Canape | 19-A |
| Relish Tray | 19-E |
| Reptile | 19-H |
| Sunflower | 19-G |
| Tomato Wedge | 19-C |

## SALAD SPREAD VARIATIONS

| | |
|---|---|
| Chicken Liver Pate | 21-K |
| Chicken Salad Canape | 21-B |
| Chopped Clam Canape | 21-F |
| Chopped Pork Canape | 21-L |
| Deviled Egg Canape | 21-H |
| Egg Salad Canape | 21-D |
| Ham Salad Canape | 21-A |
| Ham Salad and Cheese Canape | 21-E |
| Salmon Log | 21-J |
| Shrimp Salad Canape | 21-I |
| Tuna Fish Canape | 21-G |
| Tuna Salad Canape | 21-C |

## CHEESE VARIATIONS

| | |
|---|---|
| American Cheese Canape | 23-E |
| Bleu Cheese Canape | 23-A |
| Cheddar Cheese Carrot | 23-C |
| Cheddar Cheese Medley | 23-L |
| Cheese and Bacon Canape | 23-K |
| Colby Cheese Combo Canape | 23-J |
| Cream Cheese Canape | 23-G |
| French Brie Canape | 23-B |
| Mozzarella Cheese Canape | 23-I |
| Muenster Cheese Canape | 23- |
| Nut-Cheese Canape | 23- |
| Swiss Cheese Canape | 23- |

## EGG VARIATIONS

| | |
|---|---|
| Decorated Egg Canape | 25- |
| Egg and Chicken | 25- |
| Egg and Tomato | 25- |
| Egg Basket I | 25- |
| Egg Basket II | 25- |
| Jonah the Whale | 25- |
| Lady Bug | 25- |
| Perky Penguin | 25- |
| Smile | 25- |
| Sombrero | 25- |
| The Jaws | 25- |
| Tulip Time | 25- |

## MISCELLANEOUS

| | |
|---|---|
| Bacon Log with Onion | 27- |
| Big Eye | 27- |
| Biltmore | 27- |
| Canadienne | 27- |
| Deli Special | 27- |
| Herring Time | 27 |
| Medallion | 27- |
| New Yorker Canape | 27- |
| Sardine and Egg Canape | 27- |
| Sliced Turkey Canape | 27- |
| Swiss-American Canape | 27- |
| Walnut Canape | 27- |

# APPENDIX: SELECTED SAUCES

| | | | | | |
|---|---|---|---|---|---|
| Cracked Pepper Mayonnaise | 28 | Lemon Mayonnaise | 28 | Sauce Verte | 28 |
| Grated Horseradish Mayonnaise | 28 | Louis Dressing | 28 | Seasoned Cream Cheese | 28 |
| Green Peppercorn Mayonnaise | 28 | Mustard Mayonnaise | 28 | Seasoned Mayonnaise | 28 |
| Horseradish Sauce | 28 | Remoulade Sauce | 28 | **NOTES** | 29 |

# INTRODUCTION

The formula for profitable hors d'oeuvre and canape production combines the use of fully-cooked, ready-to-serve ingredients with easy-to-follow directions for their assembly. The 168 items described and pictured throughout this volume were designed to help foodservice workers turn out attractive and uniform products with a minimum of supervision. The pictures make clear exactly how each item should look; the directions make clear what steps to take for the most efficient production of each item. Fully-cooked, ready-to-serve ingredients are specified in this book to reduce production time and to minimize costly energy usage. The wide selection now available of these basic ingredients also permits cost-effective preparation of a greater variety of hors d'oeuvres and canapes.

Before production is scheduled, a group of items should be selected for preparation that will offer interesting contrast when arranged in an eye-appealing display. One way is to vary the bases for the hors d'oeuvres or canapes to be produced. Seashells may be used to hold squares of fish and other seafood hors d'oeuvres. Sliced cold meats or poultry may be shaped into cornets and stuffed with compatible fillings to become flavorful cornucopias. Among cold canapes, contrast may be achieved by varying the shapes, sizes, and materials of the bread bases. Specify rounds, squares, and fingers of white and dark breads to enhance arrangements. Another variable can be the shapes of the toppings for bread bases: level, heaped, or highlighted by a single ingredient such as a smoked oyster, a whole shrimp, or a slice of hard-cooked egg. Other base ingredients that can give a new look are vegetables such as artichoke bottoms and mushroom caps. Color—another source of variety for the displays—can come from the basic ingredients themselves, from dressings, and from garnishes. Be sure the individual hors d'oeuvres and canapes chosen for combination are flavorfully compatible, as well as colorfully pleasing.

Many of the hors d'oeuvres and canapes pictured on the following pages are shown on a bed of sparkling aspic, a background sure to successfully showcase your individual creations. Oysters and other shellfish served in the shell look their best served on crushed ice. Full flavor is assured for oysters and clams if they are opened as close as possible to serving time. Crisp parsley and neatly-cut lemon wedges spark the individual items in such a display. Placing ready-to-eat seafood in an ice carving or in large silver bowls on pedestals enhances the seafood and focuses attention on the entire hors d'oeuvre and canape array. The sauces and accompaniments that patrons enjoy with oysters, clams, shrimp, and other seafoods add separate notes of color.

For best results, an aspic coating is recommended for cold hors d'oeuvres and canapes, to preserve moistness and add highlights. Aspic for use as a coating or background must be clear and light in color. Today aspic can be made from a granulated product to meet standards dictated by its use. In using granulated apsic, follow the directions on the manufacturer's label to assure desired consistency. The aspic for individual items must provide a delicate, never rubbery coating, while aspic of a somewhat firmer consistency, such that it can be diced or chopped, is needed as a bed for display on trays or platters.

A cocktail buffet table presentation of cold hors d'oeuvres and canapes requires the preparation of sizable quantities of each item selected, as trays or platters usually hold several rows, with each row featuring one kind. For such presentations, all items of a kind must be uniform in size, shape, and appearance. The speedy assembly that quantity production requires depends on well-thought-out work stations with fully-cooked, ready-to-serve ingredients and garnishes, arranged for the most efficient and uniform combinations. Giving foodservice workers easy-to-follow directions and easy-to-duplicate pictures further assures the speedy assembly that keeps costs down and uniformity and acceptance high.

# ABOUT THE AUTHOR

Executive Chef Charles Mok learned the fundamentals of fine food preparation and presentation at the Washburne Chef Training School in Chicago, Illinois. He has perfected his art while serving as the executive chef of exclusive clubs and luxury restaurants. More recently, his responsibilities in multi-unit food organizations have focused his continuing search for practical applications of the techniques needed to provide showcase cold hors d'oeuvres and canapes.

The author also has mastered the techniques of providing preparation guides for workers who are developing their skills. His photographs lucidly illustrate the corresponding directions for preparation, and make each recipe easy to duplicate. The author's approach assures a uniformly-high level of performance among food production workers.

Charles Mok is a member of the American Academy of Chefs and the honor society of the American Culinary Federation, and is the author of the companion volume *Practical Salad and Dessert Art*.

# BASIC TOOLS FOR PREPARATION

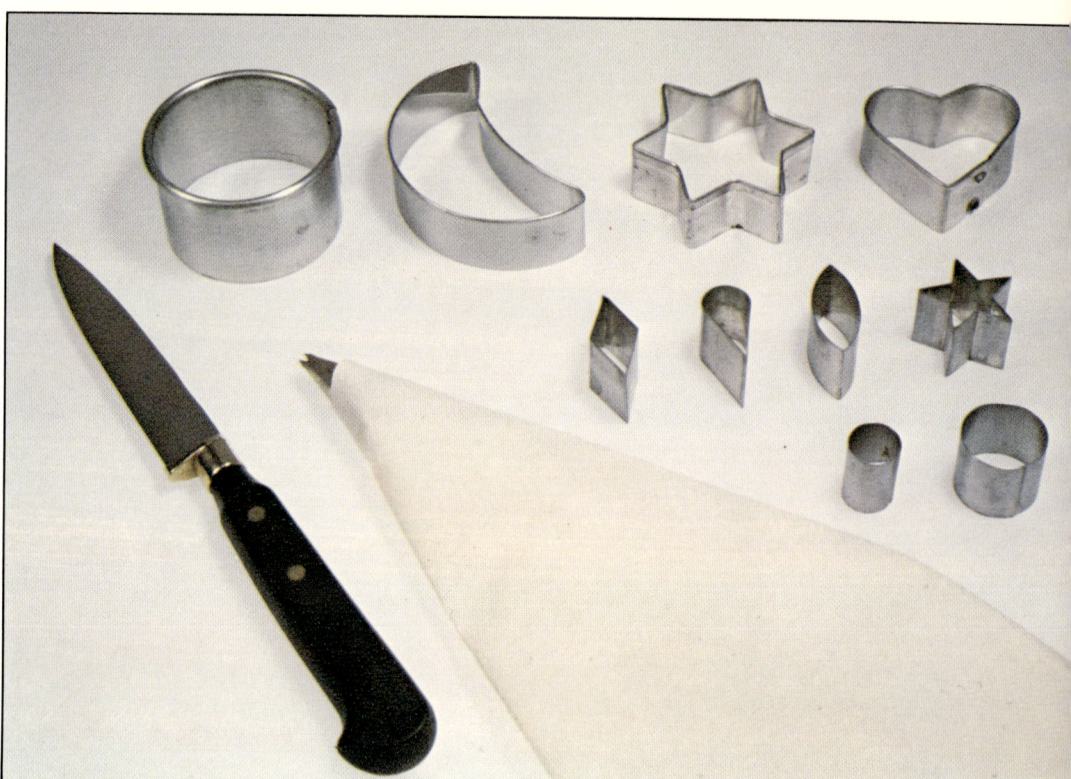

Displayed above are the basic tools required for preparation of cold hors d'oeuvres and canapes: cookie cutters, aspic cutters, a pastry bag, and a paring knife.

*FOR BEST RESULTS, COLD HORS d'OEUVRES AND CANAPÉS SHOULD BE GLAZED WITH CLEAR ASPIC.*

# BASIC INGREDIENTS CHECK LIST

## SEAFOOD ITEMS

Caviar, black
Caviar, red
Clam Meat, chopped
Clams, baby, smoked
Clams, Cherry Stone, fresh
Clams, smoked
Crab Fingers with shell
Crab Legs in shell
Crab Meat, chunks
Escargots, imported
Gefilte Fish
Herring, fillet of, in cream
Herring, large fillet in wine sauce
Lobster, chunk meat
Lobster, Rock, tails
Mussels, in shell, fresh or cooked
Oysters, fresh
Oysters, smoked
Salmon, red, cooked
Salmon, smoked thick sliced
Sardine Fillets, imported
Scallops, uncooked
Shrimp, baby
Shrimp, large
Sturgeon, smoked
Tuna, raw, imported

## MEAT AND POULTRY ITEMS

Bacon
Bacon, Canadian
Beef, Corned, cooked
Beef, cubed
Beef, Roast (rare), sliced
Beef, Sirloin, ground
Brains, Calves'
Chicken Breast, cooked
Eggs, hard-cooked
Ham, cooked, sliced
Ham, Prosciutto, sliced
Ham rolled, sliced
Headcheese
Liver, Goose, canned
Livers, Chicken
Meats, assorted cold, sliced
Pork, chopped
Sausage, Liver
Sausage, smoked
Tongue, Beef, sliced
Turkey, roast, sliced

## DAIRY ITEMS

Butter
Cheese, American
Cheese, Bleu
Cheese, Brick Cheddar
Cheese, Brie, French
Cheese, Cheddar, white & yellow
Cheese, Colby
Cheese, Cream
Cheese, Feta
Cheese, Mozzarella, shredded
Cheese, Muenster
Cheese, Swiss
Cheese Spread, Cheddar

## PRODUCE ITEMS

Artichokes
Avocadoes
Carrots
Celery
Cucumbers
Dill Weed
Grapes, dark
Lemons
Melons, Honey Dew
Mint Leaves
Mushrooms, large
Onions
Onions, Green
Parsley
Peppers, Green
Radishes
Strawberries
Tomatoes
Tomatoes, Cherry

## GROCERY ITEMS

Anchovy, fillets of
Asparagus Spears, white
Capers
Corn-on-the-Cob, miniature
Cranberry Sauce
Gelatin, clear
Mushrooms, button
Olives, black (ripe)
Olives, Greek
Olives, green
Olives, large pitted
Onions, cocktail
Orange Sections, Mandarin
Pickle Spears
Relish, sweet

## COLD HORS d'OEUVRES:

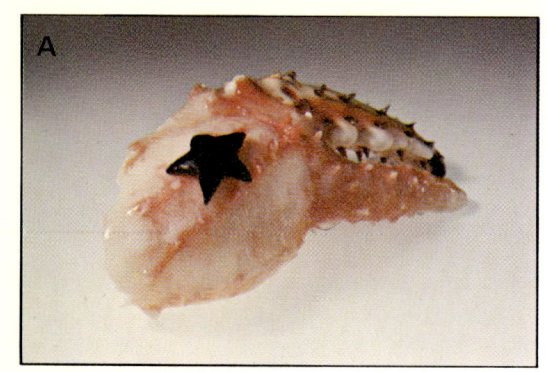

# SEAFOOD VARIATIONS

### CRAB FINGER
zen crab fingers, cooked
ange on crushed ice, shells trimmed as pur-
sed, with lemon and parsley.
UCES: Louis dressing*, cocktail sauce, green
percorn mayonnaise*, and mustard sauce.

### B  CHERRY STONE CLAM
Fresh clams
Open clams close to time of service, leaving each one on a half-shell. Arrange half-shells on crushed ice with lemon and parsley. Serve with saltines and oysterettes.
SAUCES: Cocktail sauce, grated horseradish sauce*, Worcestershire sauce, and liquid hot pepper sauce.
NOTE: Open clams carefully to prevent cutting clam. Do not open too far in advance. Keep opened clams chilled.

### C  CAVIAR CONCERT
Black caviar
Present caviar in original container.
GARNISHES: Fine-chopped egg white, fine-chopped egg yolk, fresh minced onion, and saltines or very thin rye toast.

### D  SCALLOP DELICIA
Uncooked scallops
Poach whole scallops in well-seasoned stock (white wine, thyme, onion, celery, salt, and white pepper) for approximately 8 minutes; cool. Glaze with aspic.
GARNISHES: Carrot curls and parsley.

### ESCARGOTS EN BROCHETTE
argots†
en pepper
ion
tton mushroom
ce one snail on plastic sword pick, follow with
nched green pepper square, onion square,
other snail, and end with a small button mush-
m. Marinate complete brochette in suitable
nch or Italian dressing for a few hours before
ving
TE: Rinse escargots well before forming into
chettes.

### F  RAW TUNA
Raw tuna
Cut imported tuna into 1 in.-by-½ in.-by-½ in. pieces. Arrange fish on crushed ice or chilled platter.
GARNISHES: Green pepper cut-outs, ripe olive, fine-minced onion, and soy sauce mixed with grated horseradish.

### G  OYSTER ON THE HALF SHELL
Fresh oysters
Open oysters close to time of service, arranging each on the deeper of its two half-shells. Place shells on crushed ice. Offer oysterettes along-side, with salt, pepper, grated horseradish, Worcestershire sauce, liquid hot pepper sauce, and cocktail sauce.
GARNISHES: Lemon wedge and parsley.
NOTE: Serve opened oyster in deep half-shell to retain oyster juice. Keep opened oysters chilled at all times.

### H  MUSSEL DIABLE
Fresh or cooked mussels† in shells
Open cooked mussels, retaining a half-shell for each. Place well-seasoned mustard mayonnaise* in half-shell. Arrange mussel on sauce.
GARNISHES: Hard cooked egg, lemon, and parsley.

### SHRIMP COCKTAIL
oked, peeled, deveined shrimp†
range shrimp on crushed ice or sculpted ice
ce.
RNISH: Lemon wedge.
UCES: cocktail sauce, grated horseradish
ce*, Remoulade sauce*, sauce Verte*, Louis
essing*.

### J  CLAM ROYALE
Fresh clams
Green pepper
Crisp bacon bits
Pimiento
Steam clams for 10 minutes. Remove clams from shell. Chop green pepper and pimiento. Mix wtih bacon bits in just enough mustard mayonnaise* to hold vegetables together. Put mixture in bottom of shell. Top with clam which has been dipped in well-seasoned, clear fish aspic. Arrange filled clam shells on crushed ice.

### K  MUSHROOM BUTTON GARNI
Cooked mushroom caps
Seafood salad
Remove stems from button mushrooms. Marinate caps in Italian dressing. Fill Parisienne spoon with minced seafood and drop portion into each mushroom button cavity.
GARNISHES: Radish slice design and parsley.

### L  LOBSTER MEDALLION
Cooked lobster tail
Slice lobster tail meat into ¼ in. slices. Glaze meat with clear aspic.
GARNISH: Ripe olive cut-outs.

cipe in Appendix
oduct (ingredient) available in fully-cooked, eady-to-serve stage

## COLD HORS d'OEUVRES:

# MEAT AND POULTRY VARIATIONS

## MELON CORNET
ed cold meat
on ball
am cheese

l sliced cold meat into horn or cone. Pipe
all amount of cream cheese into small end of
n. Put melon ball in large end of horn.
*RNISH:* Pipe ribbon of cream cheese along
rn edge under melon ball.

## B  SMOKED TONGUE TREAT
Cooked smoked beef tongue
Sliced tiny whole carrot

Cut beef tongue into thin slices, and cut slices into ¾ in. widths. Fold and secure tongue strips on skewer, placing a very thin slice of tiny whole carrot between each folded tongue strip. End with whole pearl onion and green pea.
*GARNISHES:* Pearl onion and green pea.

*NOTE:* Marinate brochette in suitable mild dressing for a few hours before serving.

## C  TURKEY CORNET
Turkey meat
Cream cheese
Petite orange wedge

Roll turkey meat into long horn or cone shape. Fill horn with piped cream cheese. Glaze horn with aspic. Place orange wedge on turkey as shown.
*GARNISHES:* Ripe olive cut-outs and parsley.

## D  PETITE BEEF ROULADE
Roast beef
Julienne carrot
Celery
Onion

Trim cooked beef into 1 in.-by-3 in. slices. Brush inside of beef slices with Italian dressing. Spread brushed side with sauteed, lightly seasoned julienne vegetables and pickle spears. Roll narrow side of meat slice around vegetables.
*GARNISHES:* Stuffed green olive and parsley.

## CHOPPED LIVER SURPRISE
opped chicken liver†
ead crumbs
prika

ape chicken liver into strawberry. Mix bread umbs with enough paprika to color. Cover er strawberry completely with colored crumbs.
*RNISH:* Mint leaf.

## F  HAM 'N' ASPARAGUS ROLL
Smoked ham
Cream cheese
Cooked asparagus

Sliced ham, cut into 1 in.-by-3 in. strips. Spread mustard mayonnaise* on the inside of ham strip. Roll asparagus spear in narrow width of ham slice, making certain spear tip extends beyond ham.
*GARNISHES:* Strip of cream cheese and green onion rings.

## G  CHICKEN PLANTATION
Cooked chicken meat
Swiss cheese
Sliced ham

Cut chicken meat into 1 in.-by ½ in.-by-¼ in. piece. Place a spot of thousand island dressing on chicken. Roll a smaller piece of Swiss cheese inside sliced ham strip. Place roll on top of chicken meat.
*GARNISHES:* Slice of hard-cooked egg and parsley.

## H  DELI SOMBRERO
Sliced round cold cut
Cream cheese

Make cone of center portion of cold meat slice. Fill cone with seasoned cream cheese. Fold outer edge of cold meat cone upwards to form a hat-shaped sombrero. Pipe very thin line of cream cheese around base of sombrero inside outer edge of meat.
*GARNISH:* Ripe olive cut-outs.

## CORNED BEEF SWIRL
ooked corned beef
ream cheese

ut beef into 1 in.-by-3 in. slices. Spread mixure of cream cheese, grated horseradish, and hopped parsley over inside of beef. Roll wide dge of beef slice around filling. Chill thoroughly.
*ARNISHES:* Hard-cooked egg white cut-outs nd mint leaf.

## J  MARINATED BEEF CUBE
Beef tenderloin
Cream cheese
Cucumber

Cut tenderloin into 1 in. cubes and brown on all sides. Chill and glaze with aspic. Place spot of garlic dressing on cucumber slices. Place beef cubes on sliced cucumber bases.
*GARNISHES:* Cream cheese and carrot design.

## K  MARINATED CHICKEN LIVER
Fresh chicken livers
Hard-cooked egg white

Simmer whole chicken livers in salt water until firm. Drain; cool; separate liver into 1 in. cube-shaped pieces. Marinate in light Italian dressing for a few hours. Arrange liver pieces on hard-cooked egg white cut-outs.
*GARNISHES:* Stuffed green olive half, radish slice, and parsley.

## L  STEAK TARTARE
Fresh ground sirloin of beef
Raw egg yolk
Chopped onion

Season beef with salt, pepper, and raw egg yolk and mix with fine-chopped onion. Scoop portioned mixture on petite rye round.
*GARNISHES:* Mixture of fine-chopped, hard-cooked eggs and parsley. (Capers optional.)

*NOTE:* Keep servings chilled at all times.

recipe in Appendix
product (ingredient) available in fully-cooked, ready-to-serve stage

## COLD HORS d'OEUVRES:

# EGG AND CHEESE VARIATIONS

## ANCHOVY AND EGG
d-cooked egg
lled fillet of anchovy
efully cut egg into quarters lengthwise; re-
ve yolks. Sieve yolks, mash, and season with
yonnaise, liquid hot pepper sauce, mustard,
, and white pepper. Fill quarters of hard-
ked egg white with deviled egg mixture,
ng pastry bag. Place rolled anchovy on top
stuffing.
*RNISHES:* Cherry tomato wedges and
sley.

## B ATHENEA
Greek olive
Feta cheese
Split greek olives lengthwise. Cut and trim cheese into desired portions. Place cheese on radish base. Arrange olive slices as shown.
*GARNISHES:* Cream cheese ball, green onion strips, and green pepper cut-outs.

## C MINIATURE EGG
Egg salad, fine-minced.
Add sufficient dissolved plain gelatine to spicy egg salad to make salad firm enough to shape into miniature eggs. Chill and glaze eggs with aspic. Place eggs on bed of ripe olive rings.
*GARNISHES:* Ripe olive, green onion, and pimiento strips.

## D CASPIAN EGG
Hard-cooked egg
Caviar
Cut cooked egg in half diagonally. Remove yolks and blend with seasoned mayonnaise*. Fill cavity of egg white halves with yolk-mayonnaise mixture, leaving space for caviar. Spoon caviar into this space, mounding slightly above egg half.
*GARNISHES:* Hard-cooked egg white cut-outs, stuffed olive slice, and celery leaf.
*NOTE:* Slice off tip of each egg half so it will stand as shown.

## STELLAR CHEDDAR
ck cheddar cheese
awberry
e star-shaped cutter to cut cheese stars as
wn. Glaze cheese lightly with aspic.
*RNISHES:* Strawberry halves and parsley.

## F EGG DIABLE
Hard-cooked egg
Slice hard-cooked egg in half. Remove yolk. Mash yolk and blend with chili powder, minced onion, and chopped parsley. Season with salt, pepper, mustard, and mayonnaise. Fill egg white with mixture as shown.
*GARNISHES:* Sliced radish, green onion strips, ripe olive halves and cut-outs, and cream cheese ball.

## G BLUE GEM
Bleu cheese
Artichoke bottoms
Cut bleu cheese into appropriate bite-size chunks. Place a spot of garlic mayonnaise in each artichoke bottom. Place bleu cheese chunks in mayonnaise bottom.
*GARNISHES:* Pimiento strip and green onion strips.

## H HAM AND EGGER
Hard-cooked egg
Rolled ham
American cheese
Cucumber slice
On the cucumber slice base, place dab of mustard mayonnaise*; add round slice of American cheese; top with slice of rolled ham. Cut whole hard-cooked egg into small wedges. Place one egg wedge on top of ham.
*GARNISH:* Parsley.

## STRAWBERRY DELIGHT
sh strawberry
e cheese
t Brie cheese into wedges. Remove section
the strawberry and replace with Brie wedge.
*RNISH:* Parsley.
*TE:* Select medium-size berries. Use berries of
form size for maximum appeal.

cipe in Appendix

## J BIRD OF PARADISE
Cheddar cheese spread
Cherry tomato
Shape cheddar cheese spread into bird shape. Place cheese "bird" on cherry tomato halves. Chill. Use toasted almond slices, inserted in "bird," to make wings and tail.
*GARNISHES:* Ripe olive cut-outs as eyes, and radish slice as comb.

## K KALEIDOSCOPE
Headcheese
Cucumber
Cut stripe-peeled cucumber into 1/8 in. thick slices. Put dab of cracked pepper mayonnaise* on cucumber slice. Top with circle of sliced headcheese cut to fit cucumber slice.
*GARNISHES:* Unpeeled cucumber triangles, cooked tiny whole carrot, ripe olive ring, and cream cheese.

## L STAR-TOP
Cherry tomato
Cream cheese
Walnut halves
Cut cherry tomato in half and remove seeds. Fill tomato cavity with seasoned cream cheese. Arrange toasted walnuts on cream cheese as shown.
*GARNISH:* Parsley.

## COLD HORS d'OEUVRES:

# VEGETABLE VARIATIONS

## A ARTICHOKE PHEASANT
...sh artichoke
...eddar cheese

...mer artichoke until done. Chill. Cut into 10
...2 wedges. Shape cheddar cheese spread into
...rd" and place on artichoke bottoms as shown.

...RNISHES: Radish slices and cucumber peel.

...TE: Trim bottom so that "bird" can stand
...its own.

## B WESTERN STAR
Cucumber slices
Ham salad
Cheddar cheese spread

Cut cucumber slice into star shape. Scoop ham salad ball onto center of star. Pipe cheddar cheese spread over ham salad.

GARNISHES: Cocktail onion wedges and pimiento cut-outs.

## C RADISH PLANTER
Large round radish
Julienne of vegetables

Cut off tops and roots of radish. Hollow out radish from end to end. Julienne green onion, carrot, celery, and green pepper. Insert vegetables into radish opening.

GARNISH: Ripe olive ring.

## D HEART OF PALM WITH PROSCIUTTO
Heart of palm
Prosciutto ham

Cut palm into 1 in. piece. Marinate in Italian dressing for ½ hour. Trim ham into suitable size and wrap around marinated palm.

GARNISHES: Ripe olive ring, cream cheese ball, and green pepper cut-outs.

## E HAM AND CUCUMBER WEDGE
...cumber
...ced ham

...el and split fresh cucumber lengthwise. Re-
...ve seeds. Cut into 2 in. wedges. Roll up sliced
...m; cut into 1 in. length. Place ham roll on
...cumber wedge, and season cucumber with
...ch of mustard mayonnaise*.

...RNISHES: Stuffed green olive slices, dab of
...am cheese, and carrot cut-outs.

## F STUFFED ARTICHOKE BOTTOM
Medium artichoke bottom
Chopped chicken liver

Fill artichoke bottom with seasoned chopped chicken liver. Glaze with clear aspic.

GARNISHES: Fine-chopped onion and sliced hard-cooked egg.

## G TOMATO BOAT
Tomato
Swiss cheese
Cheddar cheese spread

Cut tomato into 6 to 8 wedges. Remove seeds. Pipe cheddar cheese ball into center of wedge, making sure the ball is secure in the wedge. Cut sail out of swiss cheese slice. Place sail firmly in cheddar cheese ball.

GARNISHES: Ripe olive strips and parsley.

## H WATER CHESTNUT SURPRISE
Large water chestnut
Ham salad

Peel water chestnut; scoop top and center part out with knife. Fill center with fine-chopped ham salad. Arrange water chestnut slices in design as shown.

GARNISHES: Cream cheese and green pea.

## I CHERRY BOMB
...erry tomato
...asoned salad (as desired)

...move top and center of cherry tomato. Fill
...mato with salad of your choice. Glaze with
...pic. Place stuffed tomato on sliced ripe olive
...rcle.

...RNISHES: Green onion rings, cream cheese,
...d parsley.

## J CARROT-OLIVE STUFFER
Jumbo pitted olive
Cream cheese
Cooked carrot stick
Green olive

Remove section of olive and insert carrot stick in center. Be sure carrot stick is lightly longer than olive. Fill top part of olive with seasoned cream cheese. Place green olive cut-outs on top of cream cheese, then place arrangement on top of carrot stick.

GARNISH: Parsley.

## K MUSHROOM CAP WITH AVOCADO
Large mushroom cap
Avocado puree

Remove stem from mushroom cap. Fill cap with mixture of fine-chopped avocado and minced onion, seasoned with lemon juice, salt, and pepper, and held together with a light touch of mayonnaise. Glaze immediately with seasoned aspic.

GARNISH: Tomato wedges.

## L CELERY STUFFER
Celery rib
Seasoned cream cheese*

Scrape strings and remove leaves from fresh celery rib. Cut into 1 in. pieces. Pipe seasoned cream cheese into center of celery.

GARNISHES: Pimiento strips, stuffed olive, and parsley.

*...ecipe in Appendix

## COLD HORS d'OEUVRES:

# MISCELLANEOUS

## MUSHROOM BROCHETTE
Button mushrooms
Green peas
Place button mushroom on plastic cocktail sword with one blanched green pea inserted between each button mushroom. Marinate brochette in light vinaigrette dressing.
*GARNISH:* Natural

## B  HAM AND CUKE CAROUSEL
Ham salad
Cucumber
Peel and cut cucumber into ½ in.-thick slices. Remove seeds from center of cucumber slice. Fill center with fine-chopped ham salad shaped into round balls.
*GARNISHES:* Tomato skin rolled into rose, and celery leaf.

## C  GOOSE LIVER ROULADE
Imported goose liver (canned)
Chill can of pate thoroughly. Open both ends of cylindrical can: use one can lid to push liver out to permit slicing. Arrange slices on icing rack and coat slices with aspic.
*GARNISH:* Black olive cut-outs for design.

## D  CALVES' BRAINS SURPRISE
Large mushroom cap
Fresh calves brains
Poach calves' brains in well-seasoned stock. Chill. Trim calves' brains into uniform pieces. Glaze with aspic. Place brains in mushroom caps.
*GARNISHES:* Chopped bacon bits, radish slices, parsley, and cream cheese.

## OLIVE AND AVOCADO
Avocado
Pitted ripe olive
Cream cheese
Cut avocado into wedges. Rub lemon juice on avocado to prevent discoloration. Stuff pitted olive with seasoned cream cheese. Place stuffed olive in center of avocado wedge.
*GARNISH:* Toasted almond slices.

## F  CRAB FINGER BOAT
Crab leg in shell
Carefully split crab leg in half lengthwise. Cut into 1 to 2 in. piece. Offer cocktail sauce.
*GARNISHES:* Lemon wedge and parsley.

## G  HUNTER'S PRIDE
Brick cheddar cheese
Chicken
Ham
Cut chicken meat into 1 in. strips; cut brick cheddar into ¾ in. strips. Slice ham into pieces ½ in.-by-3 in. Place a dab of mustard mayonnaise* on chicken. Place cheese on chicken meat. Roll chicken, cheese, and ham slices together.
*GARNISH:* Stuffed green olive held in place with cocktail pick.

## H  LOX AND CREAM CHEESE
Lox
Cream cheese
Onion
Lemon slice
Slice lox, coat inside of lox with whipped cream cheese. Slice onion into julienne. Roll lox around with onion slices. Place lox roll on sliced lemon.
*GARNISHES:* Dab of cream cheese and ripe olive slice.

## PROSCIUTTO AND LEMON
Melon ball
Prosciutto ham
Hollow out center part of melon ball with sharp knife. Roll ham into round shape. Insert ham into melon ball center. Loosen top part of ham and roll to make flower design.
*GARNISH:* Parsley.

## J  TOMATO TOPPER
Cherry tomato
Mushroom cap
Fine-chopped salad
Remove seed and pulp from center of cherry tomato. Fill tomato with salad of your choice. Place mushroom cap over filled tomato.
*GARNISHES:* Stuffed olive slice and parsley.

## K  SWEETBREAD 'N' ARTICHOKE
Veal sweetbread
Artichoke
Chopped bacon bits
Poach veal sweetbread in white wine until firm. Chill. Trim sweetbread into pieces to fit center of artichoke bottom. Place sweetbread in artichoke bottom. Sprinkle bacon bits over sweetbread pieces.
*GARNISHES:* Thin cucumber slice (center removed), cream cheese, caper, and parsley.

## L  SEAFOOD DIABLE
Seafood salad
Season seafood salad with a touch of mustard and hot sauce and roll salad into portioned round balls. Place balls in scrubbed clam shells.
*GARNISHES:* Lemon wedge and parsley.

*recipe in Appendix

# COLD CANAPÉS:

# SEAFOOD VARIATIONS

**SALMON ROSE**

ked salmon or lox

salmon slice up tightly. Place roll on pre-
ed piece of toast or bread. Loosen top edge
iced salmon roll to give petal effect.

*RNISHES:* Lemon slice, parsley, and thin
es of onion.

**B  MARINATED HERRING**

Herring fillet in wine sauce

Trim fillet into bite-size portions. Place each fish portion on pre-shaped piece of toast or bread. Glaze fish with clear aspic.

*GARNISHES:* Stuffed green olive slice and celery leaf.

**C  SMOKED SALMON SPREAD**

Smoked salmon
Cream cheese

Blend fine-chopped salmon, onion, and parsley with cream cheese. Season with touch of lemon juice. Spread mixture or shape into round balls when chilled. Place mixture or ball on pre-shaped piece of toast or bread that has been covered with celery leaves.

*GARNISHES:* Sliced mushroom, celery leaves, and parsley.

**D  DEVILED CLAM**

Chopped clams

Blend clams, celery, onion, and parsley into mustard mayonnaise* to make salad. Spread salad on pre-shaped piece of toast or bread. Glaze with clear aspic.

*GARNISHES:* Pimiento strips and green peas.

**SMOKED OYSTER**

ked oyster
l onion
ish cut-out

t oyster into halves lengthwise. Place oyster
es on half-moon shaped piece of toast or
d as shown. Glaze immediately with aspic.
e a small pearl onion as head of figure; make
of radish cut-out.

*RNISHES:* Green peas and green onion
os.

**F  LOBSTER TAIL CANAPE**

Lobster tail

Poach lobster tail until firm. Chill. Slice into bite-size portion or medallion. Place lobster tail medallion on pre-shaped piece of toast or bread. Spread base with seasoned mayonnaise*. Glaze with aspic.

*GARNISH:* Design made of green onion strips, ripe olive slices, and radish strips.

**G  CRAB LOG CANAPE**

King crab leg meat

Cut crab leg meat into 1 in. portions. Place leg meat on pre-shaped piece of toast or bread that has been spread with lemon mayonnaise*. Glaze with clear aspic.

*GARNISHES:* Lemon peel, green pepper, and parsley.

**H  SMOKED BABY CLAMS**

Smoked baby clams
Pearl onion
Cream cheese

Arrange clams on pre-shaped piece of toast or bread as shown. Place small pearl onion in between clams, fastening with dab of cream cheese.

*GARNISHES:* Carrot strips and parsley.

**MARINATED GEFILTE FISH**

ilte fish

e fish into bite-size portions. Marinate por-
ns in light vinaigrette dressing. Place each fish
tion on pre-shaped piece of toast or bread
has been decorated with young celery leaves.

*RNISHES:* Cooked baby carrot slice and
olive star.

**J  SARDINE CANAPE**

Sardine
Green stuffed olive

Trim sardine so that the fish rests on its stom-
ache. Cut stuffed olive into quarters. Arrange fish and olive as shown (note position of pimiento from stuffed olive); place arrangement on thin slice of lemon.

*GARNISHES:* Parsley, American cheese cut-outs, and ripe olive bits for eyes.

**K  RED CAVIAR CANAPE**

Red caviar

Spread caper butter on pre-shaped piece of toast or bread. Pipe or arrange red caviar on canape base.

*GARNISHES:* Radish slice, caper, and parsley.

**L  JUMBO SHRIMP**

Uncooked jumbo shrimp

Peel and devein shrimp. Poach shrimp until firm. Split shrimp half-way along back. It should open up into round shape. Brush cocktail sauce on canape base. Arrange shrimp on pre-shaped piece of toast or bread as shown.

*GARNISHES:* Cherry tomato wedge and parsley.

*ipe in Appendix*

*TE: BREAD, TOAST, OR CRACKER USED FOR CANAPE BASE SHOULD BE SPREAD WITH A SUITABLE SPREAD (BUTTER, MAYONNAISE) BEFORE BEING TOPPED WITH FEATURED CANAPE INGREDIENT.*

## COLD CANAPÉS:

# SEAFOOD VARIATIONS

## SHRIMP SALAD CANAPE
imp salad (instructions below)
e-chop cooked shrimp, celery, onion, and
sley. Blend well with seasoned mayonnaise*.
ce salad on pre-shaped piece of toast or bread.
RNISHES: Green pepper strips, ripe olive,
 whole baby shrimp.

## B  TUNA SALAD CANAPE
Tuna salad
Radish slices
Prepare tuna salad. Drain well. Place thin radish slices on base (pre-shaped piece of toast or bread). Next arrange salad on base, leaving outer edges of radish slices uncovered.
GARNISHES: Stuffed green olive and celery leaves.

## C  SALMON SALAD CANAPE
Salmon salad (instructions below)
Combine red salmon with fine-chopped celery and green pepper, and blend with thousand island dressing. Drain well so that salad will not soak into bread or toast base. Arrange salad on pre-shaped piece of toast or bread.
GARNISHES: Green onion strip, radish cut-outs, and ripe olive.

## D  CRABMEAT CANAPE
Crabmeat salad (instructions below)
Combine fine-minced crabmeat with celery and parsley, and blend with small amount of whipped cream cheese. Season salad with touch of liquid hot pepper sauce and lemon juice. Arrange salad on triangle canape base.
GARNISHES: Thin slices of crabmeat, arranged as shown, and parsley.

## LOBSTER SALAD
bster salad (instructions below)
e cooked lobster meat. Combine lobster with
ted onion and whipped cream cheese. Season
h fresh lemon juice. Arrange salad on pre-
aped piece of toast or bread.
RNISHES: Dill weed and ripe olive cut-outs

## F  GEFILTE FISH CANAPE
Cooked Gefilte fish balls
Radish slices
Cut cooked small Gefilte fish balls in half. Arrange layer of grated horseradish mayonnaise* and thin slices of radish on pre-shaped piece of toast or bread. Place two fish ball halves, round sides up, on opposite corners of base.
GARNISHES: Cooked tiny whole carrot stick and parsley.

## G  ANCHOVY RING
Anchovy fillet
Hard-cooked egg
Parsley
Radish
Sprinkle chopped egg and parsley on pre-shaped piece of toast or bread. Roll anchovy fillet into tight circle. Carve out round base for rolled anchovy from medium-sized radish as shown. Place dab of seasoned cream cheese* in radish cup, and arrange rolled anchovy on cream cheese.
GARNISH: Lemon peel design.

## H  CAVIAR CANAPE
Imported caviar
Cucumber
Stripe-peel cucumber and cut into slices ¼ in. thick. Remove seeds from center of slice. Fill center with imported caviar. Spread lemon mayonnaise* on base of pre-shaped piece of toast or bread. Place filled cucumber slice on base.
GARNISHES: Egg white cut-outs and chopped egg yolk.

## LOX AND CREAM CHEESE SWIRL
oked salmon
eam cheese
ip cream cheese until soft and season with
mon juice. Spread mixture over sliced smoked
lmon. Roll up and chill. Cut roll into whirl
ces. Place whirl on pre-shaped piece of toast
bread as shown.
ARNISH: Green peas.

## J  ESCARGOT SURPRISE
Canned escargots
Sliced hard-cooked egg
Marinate escargots in Italian dressing overnight. Spread seasoned mayonnaise* on pre-shaped piece of toast or bread. Add 1 slice of hard-cooked egg. Place 1 escargot on egg slice.
GARNISHES: Pimiento strip and parsley.

## K  SMOKED STURGEON
Smoked sturgeon
Cream cheese
Trim sturgeon into 1 in.-by-½ in. pieces. Spread whipped cream cheese over entire surface of pre-shaped piece of toast or bread and top with piece of sturgeon.
GARNISHES: Pimiento strip, caper and parsley.

## L  BABY SHRIMP CANAPE
Cooked baby shrimp
Cooked carrot stick
Arrange baby shrimp of uniform size on stick of cooked carrot. Spread cocktail sauce on pre-shaped piece of toast or bread. Lay shrimp arrangement on canape base.
GARNISHES: Radish slices, parsley, and celery leaf.

ecipe in Appendix

OTE: BREAD, TOAST, OR CRACKER USED FOR CANAPE BASE SHOULD BE SPREAD WITH A SUITABLE SPREAD (BUTTER, MAYONNAISE) BEFORE BEING TOPPED WITH FEATURED CANAPE INGREDIENT.

## COLD CANAPÉS:

# MEAT AND POULTRY VARIATIONS

**BEEF AND SALAD LOG**
ed roast beef
f salad

roast beef slices into ½ in.-by-3 in. strips. ce beef trimmings and make into beef salad. l. Portion salad into bite-size balls. Wrap ed beef around salad to make log. Place beef on pre-shaped piece of toast or bread.
*RNISHES:* Green onion strips, radish cut-s, and green pepper.

**B SMOKED HAM LOG JAM**
Smoked ham
Cream cheese

Slice ham very thin; spread cream cheese over slice. Roll ham slice into cylindrical shape. Chill. Cut log into ¾ in. pieces. Arrange ham logs on pre-shaped piece of toast or bread as shown.
*GARNISH:* Strips of green onion.

**C TURKEY LILY**
Sliced turkey breast
Cheddar cheese spread
Carrot strips

Fold turkey meat into cone shape. Half-fill center of cone with whipped cheddar cheese. Insert strip of carrot into cheese as shown.
*GARNISHES:* Celery leaves and parsley.

**D SMOKED TONGUE SPECIAL**
Smoked beef tongue
Julienne of vegetables

Cut smoked tongue into 2 in. julienne strips. Combine tongue with julienne of celery, green onion, and onion. Arrange meat and vegetables in bundle. Wrap strip of blanched green onion around bundle. Spread mustard mayonnaise* on pre-shaped piece of toast or bread. Place wrapped bundle on base.
*GARNISH:* Natural

**TURKEY CLUB CANAPE**
key meat
sp bacon
tuce
rry tomato

ead pre-shaped piece of toast or bread with yonnaise. Arrange trimmed lettuce on toast read, add dot of mayonnaise. Place thin es of turkey next, add another dot of mayon-se, and position slice of cherry tomato on it. bacon until crisp; roll to round shape. Center of mayonnaise on tomato slice to hold bacon in place on top of arrangement.
*RNISH:* Parsley.
*TE:* Use pastry bag for mayonnaise.

**F SPOTTED BUTTERFLY**
Sliced cold meat
Ripe olive
Green onion
Radish slices
Stuffed olive

Trim cold meat with 2 in. round cutter. Fold meat in half. Place dab of cream cheese in center. Place meat on pre-shaped piece of toast or bread that has been spread with mayonnaise. Arrange ripe olive to make body, green onion rings for wings, radish slices as tail, and stuffed olive as head.
*GARNISH:* Green onion rings.

**G HAM AND SWISSER**
Sliced ham
Swiss cheese

Shred ham very thin. Pile ham on pre-shaped piece of toast or bread that has been lightly spread with mustard mayonnaise*. Cut swiss cheese into 1 in.-by-½ in. pieces. Arrange on base as shown.
*GARNISH:* Cucumber fan.

**H PERKY TURKEY**
Sliced turkey
Cherry tomato

Slice turkey meat very thin. Roll into round shape. Remove center part of cherry tomato with knife. Place turkey roll in tomato center. Loosen top of turkey roll to make flower petal. Place arrangement on pre-shaped piece of toast or bread.
*GARNISHES:* Capers and parsley.

**FOR LIVER LOVERS**
er sausage
edded carrot
ced onion

nd minced onion with liver sausage. Shape ture into pineapple. Sprinkle shredded carrot pre-shaped piece of toast or bread. Place liver eapple in position as shown.
*RNISH:* Mint leaf.

**J POW WOW**
Sliced turkey
Whipped cheddar cheese

Roll turkey slice into cone shape. Fill center with whipped cheddar cheese. Trim lower part of turkey so that the cone will stand up. Place cone on slice of cherry tomato. Center arrangement on pre-shaped piece of toast or bread.
*GARNISHES:* Green onion strips and radish slice at opening of cone.

**K SMOKED SAUSAGE AND SLAW**
Smoked sausage
Creamy cole slaw

Spread creamy cole slaw (well drained) on pre-shaped piece of toast or bread. Cut smoked sausage into thin slices. Arrange sausage slices on slaw as shown.
*GARNISHES:* Radish slice and ripe olive star.

**L PASTRAMI SPECIAL**
Sliced pastrami
Peeled cucumber slice
Lettuce

Slice pastrami very thin. Brush peeled cucumber slice with grated horseradish mayonnaise*. Arrange lettuce on buttered canape base. Place pile of pastrami on cucumber slice and center on base.
*GARNISHES:* Tiny whole carrot slices, ripe olive cut-outs, and lettuce for canape base decoration.

*ipe in Appendix*

*TE: BREAD, TOAST, OR CRACKER USED FOR CANAPE BASE SHOULD BE SPREAD WITH A SUITABLE SPREAD (BUTTER, MAYONNAISE) BEFORE BEING TOPPED WITH FEATURED CANAPE INGREDIENT.*

## COLD CANAPÉS:

# MEAT AND POULTRY VARIATIONS

## BAR-B-Q BEEF DELIGHT
Roast beef
Barbecue sauce
Whole onion

Slice beef very thin. Arrange in bite-size piles. Shred onion and place shreds on pre-shaped piece of toast or bread. Place piled beef over onion on canape base. Brush beef with barbecue sauce.

*GARNISHES:* Radish slice and green pepper strip.

## B  HEADCHEESE PYRAMID
Headcheese
Unpeeled cucumber slice

Shape headcheese into small pyramid shape with ¾ in. base. Place headcheese pyramid on thin cucumber slice. Brush canape base with mustard mayonnaise*. Arrange headcheese and cucumber slice on base.

*GARNISH:* Ripe olive cut-outs

## C  LIVER AND EGG
Liver sausage
Hard-cooked egg slices

Trim and slice liver sausage into bite-size portions. Place liver sausage portion on pre-shaped piece of toast or bread. Arrange egg slices on sausage as shown.

*GARNISHES:* Cocktail onion, green pea, radish slice, and ripe olive slice.

## D  HAM CANAPE
Smoked ham
Cucumber slice

Slice ham very thin. Arrange in bite-size piles. Place ham on thin slice of cucumber. Brush canape base with mustard mayonnaise*. Arrange ham and cucumber on canape base.

*GARNISHES:* Radish slices, cream cheese, and ripe olive cut-outs.

## HAM AND PICKLE ROLL
Smoked ham
Sweet pickle
Cream cheese

Slice ham thin, brush slices with whipped cream cheese. Place sweet pickle in center of ham slice. Roll ham tightly around pickle. Chill. Cut ham roll into 1 in. length. Place 1 in. ham roll on pre-shaped piece of toast or bread.

*GARNISH:* Green onion strips.

## F  PINEAPPLE AND CHICKEN
Sliced chicken
Pineapple
Cucumber

Cut cooked chicken meat into 1 in.-by-½ in. piece. Place a dab of thousand island dressing on sliced cucumber; arrange chicken meat on top of cucumber. Butter pre-shaped piece of toast or bread. Place chicken-topped cucumber slice on base. Top chicken meat with pineapple fan.

*GARNISHES:* Mint leaf and small circle of cherry tomato.

## G  TURKEY-CARROT COMBO
Sliced turkey (white meat)
Tiny whole carrot
Cranberry sauce

Cut turkey white meat slices into 1 in.-by-3 in. pieces. Brush sliced turkey with cranberry sauce. Place cooked tiny whole carrot in center of meat. Roll turkey around carrot. Arrange roll on pre-shaped piece of toast or bread.

*GARNISHES:* Radish slice, parsley, pimiento strips, cream cheese, and green pea.

## H  MEAT BALL HERO
Cooked petite meat balls
Tomato sauce
Shredded mozzarella cheese

Brush pre-shaped piece of toast or bread with tomato sauce. Sprinkle shredded cheese over canape base. Place cooked meat ball on cheese.

*GARNISHES:* Round sliced mushroom cap, green pepper strip, and pimiento.

## FANTASY OF HAM
Smoked ham
Gherkins
Cream cheese

Spread ham slice with whipped cream cheese. Place sweet gherkin in center of ham slice; roll ham around gherkin. Chill. Cut roll on the diagonal into bite-size portions, leaving one end flat. Place flat end of roll on pre-shaped piece of toast or bread.

*GARNISH:* Cream cheese piped around ham base.

## J  PIQUANT BEEF
Roast beef
Cheddar cheese spread

Slice roast beef thin. Roll beef into elongated horn or cone shape, as shown. Fill center of cone with piped-in cheddar cheese. Spread cream cheese on pre-shaped piece of toast or bread, and set horn in place in cream cheese.

*GARNISHES:* Carrot slice, ripe olive, onion rings, and parsley.

## K  PETITE SAUSAGE AND CHEESE
Petite sausage
Seasoned cream cheese*

Split petite sausage in half lengthwise. Pipe strip of seasoned cream cheese along center of the sausage half. Arrange sausage half on pre-shaped piece of toast or bread.

*GARNISHES:* Sausage rings, parsley, and radish slice.

## L  CANADIAN CAPER
Canadian bacon
Cream cheese

Slice Canadian bacon very thin, roll up into cylindrical shape. Cut cylinder into ¼ in.-thick slices. Place 1 slice on pre-shaped piece of toast or bread as shown. Pipe whipped cream cheese into center of each slice.

*GARNISHES:* Green onion ring and pearl onion.

*recipe in Appendix

*NOTE: BREAD, TOAST, OR CRACKER USED FOR CANAPE BASE SHOULD BE SPREAD WITH A SUITABLE SPREAD (BUTTER, MAYONNAISE) BEFORE BEING TOPPED WITH FEATURED CANAPE INGREDIENT.*

# COLD CANAPÉS:

# VEGETABLE VARIATIONS

## A  PRINCESS CANAPE
White asparagus spear
Sliced ham
Cheddar cheese spread

Cut white asparagus spear into three 1-in. lengths. Wrap very thin strip of sliced ham around one length of asparagus only. Spread canape base with cheddar cheese spread. Place two naked lengths of asparagus on pre-shaped piece of toast or bread. Put ham-wrapped length on top as shown.
*GARNISHES:* Pimiento strip and parsley.

## B  ARTICHOKE BOTTOM ST. GERMAIN
Artichoke bottom
Split pea puree

Trim artichoke bottom so it will lie flat on canape base. Fill artichoke bottom with cold puree of green pea (well seasoned). Spread pre-shaped piece of toast or bread, lightly with butter or mayonnaise. Place filled artichoke on base.
*GARNISHES:* Pimiento strip, dab of cream cheese, green pea, and parsley.

## C  TOMATO WEDGE
Cherry tomato
Cream cheese
Sliced American cheese

Cut cherry tomato into wedges. Remove seeds. Fill wedge with whipped cream cheese. Spread pre-shaped canape base with mayonnaise. Place identical sized slice of American cheese on base. Arrange tomato and olive circle on cheese as shown. Place filled tomato wedge on ripe olive circle.
*GARNISH:* Ripe olive design.

## D  ALMONDINE
Toasted almond slices
Seasoned cream cheese*
Cherry tomato

Pipe seasoned cream cheese around pre-shaped canape base. Place cherry tomato cap in center of canape. Arrange toasted almond slices on cream cheese around edge of canape as shown.
*GARNISH:* Natural.

## E  RELISH TRAY
Cucumber
Stuffed olive
Radish
Cheddar cheese spread
Stuffed olive

Remove seeds from unpeeled cucumber slice. Fill center with cheddar cheese spread. Place slice on pre-shaped piece of toast or bread. Slice radish thin. Arrange slices in circle around cheese as shown.
*GARNISH:* Stuffed olive slice.

## F  CORN CRIB
Miniature corn-on-the-cob
Seasoned cream cheese*

Slice each ear of corn in half lengthwise. Pipe seasoned cream cheese on pre-shaped piece of toast or bread. Position corn as shown.
*GARNISHES:* Cherry tomato wedge and parsley.

## G  SUNFLOWER
Cherry tomato
Ripe olive
Cream cheese

Carve cherry tomato into sunflower. Remove seeds. Spread pre-shaped piece of toast or bread with cream cheese. Slice top from large, pitted ripe olive. Fill center of pitted olive with whipped cream cheese. Insert olive in tomato, and position tomato in cream cheese canape base. Replace top on cheese-filled ripe olive.
*GARNISH:* Parsley.

## H  REPTILE
Cashew nuts
Cream cheese
Onion

Blend cream cheese with fine-grated onion. Pipe cream cheese over pre-shaped toast or bread canape base, leaving mound in center. Arrange cashew nuts on cheese as shown.
*GARNISH:* Natural.

## I  NORMANDY
Asparagus tips
Cherry tomato
Cream cheese

Cook and slice asparagus tips into 1 in. lengths. Marinate tips in Italian dressing. Arrange tips on sliced tomato ring. Pipe ribbon of cream cheese over asparagus tips. Place tomato-asparagus arrangement on pre-shaped piece of toast or bread.
*GARNISH:* Asparagus slices.

## J  MUSHROOMIQUE
Mushroom cap
Radish
Cream cheese

Cut mushroom cap and radish into wedges. Marinate in light Italian dressing. On a pre-shaped piece of toast or bread, arrange mushroom and radish wedges as shown. Pipe ribbon of cream cheese over mushroom-radish arrangement.
*GARNISH:* Green onion circle.

## K  AVOCADO TERRACE
Avocado
Lemon juice
Cherry tomato
Cream cheese

Slice avocado into thin wedges; rub wedges with lemon juice and drain. Cut cherry tomato in half, remove center, and carve each half into sunflower. Position tomato and avocado, as shown, on pre-shaped piece of toast or bread. Fill tomato half with whipped cream cheese.
*GARNISH:* Natural.

## L  CARROTIQUE
Tiny whole carrot
Cream cheese
Thick radish slice

Cut cooked, tiny whole carrot in half, then into thin strips. Pipe whipped cream cheese onto thick radish slice. Arrange carrot strips on cream cheese in cone shape. Place radish slice with carrot cone on pre-shaped piece of toast or bread.
*GARNISH:* Parsley.

*recipe in Appendix

**NOTE:** *BREAD, TOAST, OR CRACKER USED FOR CANAPE BASE SHOULD BE SPREAD WITH A SUITABLE SPREAD (BUTTER, MAYONNAISE) BEFORE BEING TOPPED WITH FEATURED CANAPE INGREDIENT.*

## COLD CANAPÉS:

# SALAD SPREAD VARIATIONS

## HAM SALAD CANAPE
m salad
ion ring
son fine-chopped ham salad with touch of ted horseradish. Fill center of small onion ring h ham salad. Arrange ring on pre-shaped piece toast or bread.
*RNISH:* Ripe olive cut-outs.

## B CHICKEN SALAD CANAPE
Chicken salad
Shape fine-chopped chicken salad (well drained) into chicken; position on pre-shaped piece of toast or bread. Chill. Glaze immediately with aspic.
*GARNISHES:* Radish slices as wings and comb; parsley, and green peas.

## C TUNA SALAD CANAPE
Tuna salad
Hard-cooked egg slices
Shape well-drained tuna salad into a long cylinder no larger than an egg; cut into ¾ in.-long portions. Place portion lengthwise on unpeeled cucumber slice on pre-shaped piece of toast or bread. Add small slice of hard-cooked egg to each end of tuna salad portion.
*GARNISHES:* Lemon peel and ripe olive cut-outs.

## D EGG SALAD CANAPE
Egg salad
Ripe olive
Thoroughly blend fine-chopped egg salad with dissolved gelatin. Chill. Shape salad into miniature egg and position on thick, ripe olive ring. Place arrangement on pre-shaped piece of toast or bread.
*GARNISHES:* Sliced carrot design and olive cut-outs as shown.

## HAM SALAD AND CHEESE CANAPE
m salad
eddar cheese spread
ll fine-chopped, well-drained ham salad into inder shape smaller than base selected to hold Cut cylinder of salad into ½ in. rolls. Spread hipped cream cheese on pre-shaped piece of ast or bread. Place ham salad roll, flat end up, cheese.
*RNISH:* Cherry tomato cap.

## F CHOPPED CLAM CANAPE
Chopped clams
Cream cheese
Radish slices
Blend chopped clams, smoked or cooked, into whipped cream cheese and season with mustard. Roll mixture into balls. Place ball on thin slice of radish. Position ball and radish on pre-shaped piece of toast or bread.
*GARNISHES:* Baby clam, parsley, and ripe olive cut-out.

## G TUNA FISH CANAPE
Tuna salad
Add enough dissolved gelatin to tuna salad so it can be molded into fish shape; chill. Shape salad into fish as shown. Place fish on pre-shaped piece of toast or bread.
*GARNISHES:* Radish slices, green onion strip, and capers.

## H DEVILED EGG CANAPE
Hard-cooked egg
Capers
Cut egg in half at angle; remove yolk. Blend chopped egg yolk with mustard mayonnaise* Season well. Replace yolk with deviled egg mix. Trim egg bottom so that it will stand on pre-shaped piece of toast or bread.
*GARNISHES:* Capers, ripe olive cut-outs, and parsley.

## SHRIMP SALAD CANAPE
hrimp salad
oll well-drained shrimp salad into round ball. ace shrimp ball on pre-shaped piece of toast or read.
*ARNISHES:* Green onion strip, green pepper esign, and dab of cream cheese.

## J SALMON LOG
Salmon salad
Potato chip crumbs
Roll and shape well-drained, fine-minced red salmon salad into 1 in.-by-¼ in. logs. Roll logs in fine-crumbled potato chips. Arrange logs as shown on pre-shaped piece of toast or bread.
*GARNISH:* Parsley.

## K CHICKEN LIVER PATE
Chopped chicken liver
Onion ring
Make chopped chicken liver into pate. Slice small onion into ¼ in.-thick rings, and place chopped liver in center of onion ring. Place arrangement on pre-shaped piece of toast or bread.
*GARNISHES:* Chopped hard-cooked egg and parsley.

## L CHOPPED PORK CANAPE
Chopped cold smoked pork
Trim chopped smoked pork with cutter to bite-size portion. Spread grated horseradish mayonnaise* over pre-shaped piece of toast or bread. Arrange meat as shown.
*GARNISHES:* Green peas, pork slices, and pearl onions.

*ecipe in Appendix*

**OTE:** *BREAD, TOAST, OR CRACKER USED FOR CANAPE BASE SHOULD BE SPREAD WITH A SUITABLE SPREAD (BUTTER, MAYONNAISE) BEFORE BEING TOPPED WITH FEATURED CANAPE INGREDIENT.*

## COLD CANAPÉS:

# CHEESE VARIATIONS

**BLEU CHEESE CANAPE**
u cheese
ted ripe olive
ce pitted olive into three sections. Cut bleu
eese same size as olive sections and place be-
een olive sections. Arrange on pre-shaped
ce of toast or bread as shown.
*RNISH:* Cherry tomato wedges.

**B  FRENCH BRIE CANAPE**
French brie
Mandarin orange segments
Cut brie cheese into bite-size wedges. Arrange cheese wedges on pre-shaped piece of toast or bread, with mandarin orange segments on either side.
*GARNISHES:* Pimiento cut-outs and parsley.

**C  CHEDDAR CHEESE CARROT**
Cheddar cheese spread
Form cheddar cheese spread into carrot shape. Arrange on pre-shaped piece of toast or bread.
*GARNISHES:* Mint leaf and parsley.

**D  MUENSTER CHEESE CANAPE**
Muenster cheese
Cut cheese with almond-shaped cutter. Arrange cheese as shown. Lightly spread mayonnaise over pre-shaped piece of toast or bread. Position cheese arrangement on canape base.
*GARNISH:* Cut-outs from ends of ripe olive.

**AMERICAN CHEESE CANAPE**
ced American cheese
t cheese into slices ½ in.-square. Stack slices
top of each other at angles shown. Place
ck on pre-shaped piece of toast or bread.
*RNISH:* Stuffed olive circle.

**F  SWISS CHEESE CANAPE**
Swiss cheese
Cherry tomato
Cut cheese into triangle shape. Arrange cheese triangle with cherry tomato wedges as shown. Place arrangement on pre-shaped piece of toast or bread.
*GARNISH:* Parsley.

**G  CREAM CHEESE CANAPE**
Cream cheese
Crushed pineapple
Whip cream cheese; season with crushed pineapple. Pipe mixture on pre-shaped piece of toast or bread.
*GARNISHES:* Pineapple fan, pimiento cut-outs, and ripe olive cut-outs design.

**H  NUT-CHEESE CANAPE**
Cheddar cheese spread
Chopped nuts
Shape cheese into form of apple. Roll cheese "apple" in chopped nuts. Spread layer of cheese on pre-shaped piece of toast or bread, and position "apple" in cheese on canape base.
*GARNISHES:* Parsley with stem and pimiento strips.

**MOZZARELLA CHEESE CANAPE**
zzarella cheese
am cheese
lnuts
t and slice mozzarella cheese into same size as
ape base. Place cheese on pre-shaped toast or
ad that has been spread with mayonnaise.
e dab of cream cheese on mozzarella slice,
d decorate cream cheese with walnuts.
*RNISHES:* Green and red pepper strips.

**J  COLBY CHEESE COMBO CANAPE**
Colby cheese
Ham
Unpeeled cucumber
Cream cheese
Slice ham and cut into same size as canape base. Position ham on top with dot of cream cheese. Cut cucumber and colby cheese into thin wedges and arrange on ham as shown. Pipe dab of cream cheese in center of canape.
*GARNISH:* Ripe olive.

**K  CHEESE AND BACON CANAPE**
Chedder cheese spread
Bacon strip
Cucumber
Stripe-peel cucumber; slice. Remove seeds from center of cucumber slice; replace with cheddar cheese spread. Place cucumber slice on pre-shaped piece of toast or bread. Crisp-fry bacon and roll up. Place bacon roll on cheese spread in center of cucumber slice.
*GARNISH:* Parsley.

**L  CHEDDAR CHEESE MEDLEY**
Cheddar cheese, yellow and white
Cut both yellow and white cheddar cheese into wedges of equal size. Arrange wedges as shown on pre-shaped piece of toast or bread spread with mayonnaise.
*GARNISH:* Parsley.

*TE: BREAD, TOAST, OR CRACKER USED FOR CANAPE BASE SHOULD BE SPREAD WITH A SUITABLE SPREAD (BUTTER, MAYONNAISE) BEFORE BEING TOPPED WITH FEATURED CANAPE INGREDIENT.*

## COLD CANAPÉS:

# EGG VARIATIONS

## PERKY PENGUIN
opped hard-cooked egg white
eam cheese
pe olive

nd chopped egg white with whipped cream eese. Form mixture in miniature egg shape; ll. Arrange miniature egg on pre-shaped piece toast or bread as shown.

*RNISHES:* Ripe olive cut-outs as wings, head, d feet. Pimiento strip around neck to form tie. ts of chopped egg white for eyes, nose, and uth.

## B  THE JAWS
Hard-cooked egg
Cheddar cheese
Carrot curl

Cut egg in half at an angle. Place cut side of egg half on pre-shaped piece of toast or bread; hold in place with cream cheese. Carve another piece from egg half to form mouth. Pipe cheddar cheese into "mouth", and insert carrot curl as tongue.

*GARNISHES:* Pimiento cut-outs, capers, and cream cheese.

## C  SMILE
Hard-cooked egg
Cherry tomato

Trim egg at each end so it can stand on pre-shaped piece of toast or bread. Glaze egg immediately; chill. Use ripe olive cut-outs as eyes, mouth, and nose.

*GARNISHES:* Cherry tomato wedges and cap.

## D  LADY BUG
Hard-cooked eggs
Ripe olive half
Cream cheese

Cut hard-cooked eggs into halves lengthwise. Place cut side down on pre-shaped piece of toast or bread spread with seasoned mayonnaise*. Affix ripe olive half as head, using piped cream cheese.

*GARNISHES:* Green peas, pimiento strips, and olive cut-outs.

## DECORATED EGG CANAPE
rd-cooked egg
asted almond
eam cheese

t egg in half. Place cut side down on pre-aped piece of toast or bread. Pipe whipped am cheese around bottom of egg. Arrange asted, sliced almonds in cream cheese around g as shown.

*RNISHES:* Green pepper cut-outs, pimiento t, and ripe olive half-circles.

## F  TULIP TIME
Hard-cooked egg
Tiny whole carrot

Cut egg in half. Carve round end of egg half into tulip shape. Place egg with cut-side down on pre-shaped piece of toast or bread. Arrange thin slices of tiny whole carrot in sunflower design.

*GARNISHES:* Green onion strips, radish slices, and ripe olive.

## G  JONAH THE WHALE
Hard-cooked egg

Cut egg in half lengthwise. Place each half with cut side down on pre-shaped piece of toast or bread. Glaze immediately with aspic.

*GARNISHES:* Pimiento strip design, green onion strip, green pea, and capers.

## H  SOMBRERO
Hard-cooked egg
Stuffed olive slice
Mandarin orange segments

Cut egg in half. Place cut side down on pre-shaped piece of toast or bread. Decorate egg with stuffed olive slices and mandarin orange segments.

*GARNISHES:* Cream cheese, green pea, and green pepper cut-outs.

## EGG BASKET I
rd-cooked egg
eam cheese

rve hard-cooked egg into basket in upright sition. Remove egg yolk. Position egg in am cheese on pre-shaped piece of toast or ead. Fill inside of basket with various veg-bles.

*RNISH:* Natural

## J  EGG BASKET II
Hard-cooked egg
Cream cheese

Carve hard-cooked egg lengthwise into basket, as shown. Remove egg yolk. Position egg in cream cheese on pre-shaped piece of toast or bread. Fill inside of basket with various vegetables.

*GARNISH:* Natural

## K  EGG AND CHICKEN
Hard-cooked egg
Cheddar cheese spread
American cheese
Carrot
Green pepper

Cut egg in half. Place cut side down on pre-shaped piece of toast or bread. Shape cheddar cheese spread to form upper part of chicken. Carve green pepper as tail, carrot as comb, and American cheese triangles as wings; position as shown.

*GARNISHES:* Ripe olive cut-outs as eyes. Radish slice, green onion rings.

## L  EGG AND TOMATO
Hard-cooked egg
Cherry tomato
Cheddar cheese ball
Sliced unpeeled cucumber

Cut egg in half lengthwise. Remove yolk. Carve cherry tomato into sunflower, remove all seeds, and refill with cheddar cheese ball. Place sunflower in cavity in egg white half. Put slice of cucumber on pre-shaped piece of toast or bread. Position arrangement as shown.

*GARNISHES:* Ripe olive cut-outs, ripe-olive ring, cream cheese and parsley.

cipe in Appendix

TE: *BREAD, TOAST, OR CRACKER USED FOR CANAPE BASE SHOULD BE SPREAD WITH A SUITABLE SPREAD (BUTTER, MAYONNAISE) BEFORE BEING TOPPED WITH FEATURED CANAPE INGREDIENT.*

## COLD CANAPÉS:

# MISCELLANEOUS

## SARDINE AND EGG CANAPE
let of sardine
rd-cooked egg slices
eam cheese

range sardine in upright position. Place slice hard-cooked egg on pre-shaped piece of toast bread that has been spread lightly with lemon yonnaise*. Position fish between half-slices egg as shown. Decorate fish with piped border cream cheese.
*RNISHES:* Pimiento strips and parsley at tail.

## B  NEW YORKER CANAPE
Roast beef

Slice and trim roast beef to 1 in.-by-3 in. strips. Season canape base with horseradish mayonnaise*. Fold beef as shown and place on pre-shaped piece of toast or bread base.
*GARNISHES:* Green onion ring, cream cheese, and small cheddar cheese triangles.

## C  BILTMORE
Crisp bacon
Lettuce
Cherry tomato

Cut cherry tomato in half. Remove seeds and refill with chopped bacon bits. Spread pre-shaped piece of toast or bread with seasoned mayonnaise*. Top with shredded lettuce. Place stuffed tomato on lettuce. Place a crisp bacon roll on tomato for decoration.
*GARNISH:* Strip of onion ring.

## D  SWISS-AMERICAN CANAPE
Swiss cheese
American cheese
Cream cheese

Cut Swiss and American cheese with almond-shaped cutter. Brush mustard mayonnaise* on pre-shaped piece of toast or bread. Arrange cheese to form design on canape base as shown. Pipe dab of cream cheese in center of canape.
*GARNISH:* Parsley.

## SLICED TURKEY CANAPE
ced turkey
ndarin orange segments

ce turkey thin and roll into bite-size portions. ce two segments of orange on pre-shaped ce of toast or bread. Top with turkey roll.
*RNISHES:* Celery leaves and ripe olive cutts.

## F  DELI SPECIAL
Sliced cold meat

Cut round from cold meat slice. Cut round in half. Lightly spread pre-shaped piece of toast or bread with mustard mayonnaise*. Place unpeeled cucumber slice on base. Position half-round of meat as shown.
*GARNISH:* Pimiento strip.

## G  BIG EYE
Artichoke bottom
Cherry tomato
Fillet of anchovy

Spread lemon mayonnaise* on pre-shaped piece of toast or bread. Place a medium slice of cherry tomato on canape base; top with small artichoke bottom. Roll up anchovy fillet and place on artichoke bottom.
*GARNISHES:* Parsley, cream cheese, and capers.

## H  CANADIENNE
Canadian bacon
Cream cheese

Cut sliced Canadian bacon into same size as canape base. Roll other thin slices of Canadian bacon into cone shapes and stuff with seasoned cream cheese. Place Canadian bacon slice on pre-shaped piece of toast or bread, and arrange stuffed cones as shown.
*GARNISH:* Parsley.

## HERRING TIME
let of herring in cream
y whole carrot

m herring into bite-size portions. Arrange fish rtion on pre-shaped piece of toast or bread. corate with design of thin-sliced tiny whole rot.
*RNISHES:* Ripe olive circle and cream eese.

## J  MEDALLION
Smoked ham
Artichoke bottom

Quarter artichoke bottom. Trim thick slice of ham to same size as canape base. Lightly spread canape base with mustard mayonnaise*. Arrange meat and artichoke quarter on base as shown.
*GARNISHES:* Ripe olive stars and green pepper strip.

## K  BACON LOG WITH ONION
Chopped bacon bits
Seasoned cream cheese*

Pipe seasoned cream cheese on pre-shaped piece of toast or bread. Roll bacon bits with enough prepared mustard to hold together in long log. Position log on canape base.
*GARNISHES:* Sliced onion strips and parsley.

## L  WALNUT CANAPE
Whole and chopped walnuts
Cream cheese

Spread whipped cream cheese on pre-shaped piece of toast or bread. Sprinkle with chopped walnuts. Place a dab of cream cheese in center of canape. Arrange two whole walnut pieces on either side of cream cheese mound.
*GARNISH:* Natural.

cipe in Appendix

TE: BREAD, TOAST, OR CRACKER USED FOR CANAPE BASE SHOULD BE SPREAD WITH A SUITABLE SPREAD (BUTTER, MAYONNAISE) BEFORE BEING TOPPED WITH FEATURED CANAPE INGREDIENT.

# APPENDIX: SELECTED SAUCES

### CRACKED PEPPER MAYONNAISE— 1 gallon (plus)
Cracked Whole Black Pepper — ¼ cup
Parsley, chopped — ¼ cup
Mayonnaise — 1 gal.
Blend well, together
*KEEP CHILLED*

### GRATED HORSERADISH MAYONNAISE — 1 gallon (plus)
Horseradish, grated — 1-½ cup
Mayonnaise — 1 gal.
Squeeze vinegar out of horseradish. Add mayonnaise. Season to taste with salt and white vinegar.
*KEEP CHILLED*

### GREEN PEPPERCORN MAYONNAISE — 1 gallon (plus)
Whole green peppercorns — 1 cup
Mayonnaise — 1 gal.
Chop peppercorns coarsely with french knife and fold into mayonnaise.
*KEEP CHILLED*

### HORSERADISH SAUCE
Use Grated Horseradish Mayonnaise formula, substituting 3 quarts of cold water for 3 quarts of Mayonnaise. Mix well. Use cold or heated.

### LEMON MAYONNAISE — 1 gallon (plus)
Lemon Juice — 1 cup
Lemon Rind, grated — ¼ cup
Sugar, granulated — 1 cup
Mayonnaise — 1 gal.
Combine all. Stir thoroughly until well blended. Add to mayonnaise while whipping at medium speed.
*KEEP CHILLED*

### LOUIS DRESSING — 1 gallon (plus)
Chili Sauce — 1 pint
Tomato Catsup — 1 pint
French Dressing (homog) — 1 pint
Worcestershire Sauce — ¼ cup
Mayonnaise — 2-½ qts.
Mix all together until well blended.
*KEEP CHILLED*

### MUSTARD MAYONNAISE— 1 gallon (plus)
Dry Mustard — ¼ cup
White Wine — ⅔ cup
Orange Juice — ⅔ cup
Mayonnaise — 1 gal.
Heat wine and orange juice in double boiler. Dissolve mustard in liquid. Pour into mayonnaise while whipping.
*KEEP CHILLED*

### REMOULADE SAUCE — 1 gallon (plus)
Capers — ½ cup
Dill pickles, chopped — 1 pint
Parsley, chopped — 2 Tbs.
Chives, chopped — 2 Tbs.
Chervil — 2 Tbs.
Creole Mustard — 1 cup
Anchovy Paste — ¼ cup (optional)
Mayonnaise — 1 gal.
Chop capers, pickles, parsley, chives, and chervil very fine, together. Add mustard, anchovy paste, and mustard; whip all together.
*KEEP CHILLED*

### SAUCE VERTE — 1 gallon (plus)
Fresh Spinach, trimmed — 3 lbs. (thoroughly washed, drained)
Chives, fresh, chopped — 1 cup
Tarragon Leaves — ¼ cup
Chervil — ¼ cup
Mayonnaise — 1 gal.
Blend spinach, chives, tarragon, and chervil in electric blender until very fine. Pour into cheese cloth; squeeze juice into small double boiler. Reserve paste. Heat juice until solids separate from liquids. Strain heated materials and paste through cheese cloth, discarding liquid. Fold strained paste into mayonnaise. Season to taste with fine-minced parsley, chervil, chives and tarragon.
*KEEP CHILLED*

### SEASONED CREAM CHEESE
Cream Cheese — 3 lb. loaf
Lime Juice — ½ cup
Salt — to taste
White Pepper — to taste
Worcestershire Sauce — 1 Tbs.
Blend together.
*KEEP CHILLED.*

### SEASONED MAYONNAISE — 1 gallon (plus)
Paprika — 2 tsp.
Tarragon Leaves — 1 tsp.
Chervil, chopped — 1 tsp.
Chives, chopped — 2 Tbs.
Curry Powder — 1 tsp.
Lemon Juice — ½ cup
Sugar, granulated — ½ cup
Mayonnaise — 1 gal.
Combine all. Stir thoroughly until well blended. Add to mayonnaise while whipping at medium speed.
*KEEP CHILLED*

# NOTES

# NOTES